DATE DUE

The Israeli Communist Party

HOOVER INSTITUTION STUDIES: 9

The Israeli Communist Party

AND THE
ELECTIONS FOR THE FIFTH
KNESSET, 1961

Moshe M. Czudnowski and Jacob M. Landau

The Hoover Institution
on War, Revolution, and Peace
Stanford University, 1965

The Hoover Institution on War, Revolution, and Peace, founded at Stanford University in 1919 by Herbert Hoover, is a center for advanced study and research on public and international affairs in the twentieth century. The views expressed in its publications are entirely those of the authors and do not necessarily reflect the views of the Hoover Institution.

CONTENTS

Page

INTRODUCTION 1

PART I.   HISTORICAL BACKGROUND 4

PART II. COMPOSITION OF THE PARTY 13

          Structure 13

          Ethnic Composition 15

          Composition According to Length of
          Residence 17

          Age Composition 18

          Composition According to Land of
          Origin 19

          Educational and Occupational
          Composition 22

          The Leadership 23

PART III. MAJOR POLITICAL POSITIONS AND
          MEANS OF PROPAGANDA 27

          Conflicting Positions toward Israel .. 27

          Israel-Arab Relations 29

          Foreign Policy 30

v

Page

The Social and Economic System 31

Relations with Minorities 32

Propaganda Means 32

PART IV. ORGANIZATION AND PROPAGANDA ON
THE EVE OF THE 1961 ELECTIONS 35

Subjects Stressed for Jews 37

Subjects Stressed for Arabs 39

Subjects Stressed for Both Jews and
Arabs 40

PART V. THE ELECTIONS OF AUGUST 15, 1961 .. 42

The Total Communist Vote 42

The Communist Vote in Purely Arab
Localities 43

The Arab Communist Vote in Mixed
Localities 56

The Patterns of the Jewish Communist
Vote 63

CONCLUSIONS 87

NOTES 92

vi

INTRODUCTION*

The Fourth Knesset (Israel's legislative assembly)[1]
was dissolved prematurely before the expiration of its regular four-year term, which had begun on November 3, 1959.
Elections for the Fifth Knesset, held on August 15, 1961,[2]
resulted in a slight decline for MAPAI--the dominant mod-
erate Israel Labor Party; some gains for the center-right
Liberal Party; and a sharp, 54 per cent increase in the
popular vote for the Communist Party of Israel, popularly
known as MAQI (from the initials of its Hebrew name--
Miflaga qomūnisṭit Isre'elīt), from 27,374 to 42,111 votes.[3]

In this book, we seek to describe and analyze the
reasons for this increase in Communist strength. At the
time of writing, summer 1963, no official publications

---

*Although Dr. Landau worked mainly on the Arab
element in the Israeli Communist Party and the party's
support in the Arab sector, and Dr. Czudnowski mainly on
the Jewish element and on the party's support in the mixed
cities and in the Jewish localities, this book has been written jointly as the result of a stimulating collaboration and
both authors assume responsibility for the whole text.

detailing the election results were yet available.[4] Hence,

we limited this book to an attempt to describe the charac-

teristic tendencies of the Communist Party on the Israeli

political scene in 1961. This study has also been affected

in no small measure by the nearly conspiratorial character

of this party. These difficulties have precluded the employ-

ment of the more refined tools of political sociology and

election studies in evaluating the activities of a Communist

party in a Western-type political regime.

The Israeli Communist Party cannot be compared to

those in Western Europe nor to the Communist parties in

new states, nor even to those in territories still seeking

political independence. Whereas West European Communist

parties base their appeal largely on the socioeconomic

struggle, and Communist parties in developing or new states

support the nationalist movements of the majority of the

populations of these countries and have even attempted to

place themselves at the head of such movements, the Israeli

Communist Party is unique in that its tactics are largely

molded by deference to the nationalist tendencies of an eth-

nic and religious minority--the Arabs. This feature also

2

divides the Communists from the other parties in the State of Israel, which, even when they include Arabs in their ranks and represent their interests, concentrate on and draw their principal support from the Jewish community and identify themselves with the realization of the Zionist ideal. MAQI claims to represent Arab nationalist interests, while at the same time ignoring or even opposing the nationalist interests of the Jewish population, as interpreted by other Israeli parties representing the quasi-totality of the Jewish public. MAQI, of course, claims that it does not fail in its duty toward the proper or true interests of the Jewish community. It is forced, therefore, to employ the choicest parts of the vocabulary of Marxist-Leninist dialectics in its endeavor to reconcile the contradictions that undermine its position.

I. HISTORICAL BACKGROUND

MAQI bore the imprint of two contrasts from the very beginning: the attempt to involve, on one hand, Jews and Arabs in one party against the background of two ethnic communities torn apart by their respective nationalist tendencies; and on the other hand, the incompatibility of Communism and the Zionism of the Jewish community, within which the party also desired to win souls.

Communism appeared in Palestine[5] just after the Bolshevik Revolution in Russia within the extreme-left Socialist Zionist groups in Palestine. It first organized as the Socialist Workers Party in 1919; two years later the organization adopted the name Palestine Communist Party (P.C.P.); and in 1924 it affiliated with the Comintern. Little is known about its early structure and the social background of the leaders and the rank and file. During the British Mandate, the movement was banned (until the Soviet Union became an ally of Great Britain during the Second World War), and Communist activities were performed underground under various disguises. Furthermore, because of the absence of regular political elections on a country-wide basis involving both Jews and Arabs, little trustworthy evidence is available on the strength of the P.C.P. In elections to the Asefat ha-Nivḥarīm (the representative assembly of the organized Jewish community during the Mandate), the Communists received 1,028 votes (out of 36,690) in 1925, and 524 votes (out of 50,436) in 1931.[6]

In the face of incomplete data, one can merely indicate the following broad trends in the history of the Palestine Communist Party under the Mandate:

1. The nucleus of Jewish Communists failed in its effort to penetrate the Palestine Jewish community because of the latter's longing to realize the Zionist ideal after the Balfour Declaration and the award of the Mandate to Great Britain with the purpose of fostering a Jewish National Home. A few extreme Jewish socialists, incapable of bridging the contradiction between Communism and Zionism, soon left Palestine and settled in the Soviet Union.

2. Within the Arab community[7] conditions were not ripe for the reception of Communist ideology: feudal landlords, on the one hand, and religion and its institutions, on the other, exercised great influence. Another hurdle was raised during the thirties and the forties when nationalist ideas began to percolate among Palestinian Arabs, thus further impeding the spread of Communist ideas.

3. The limited response of Palestinian Jewry and the small size of this community persuaded Moscow to concentrate its activities among the Arabs (this paralleled a growing Soviet interest in the Arab countries generally). This shift in policy was easy to coordinate, ideologically, with the struggle against the British regime launched by the leaders of the Palestine Arabs. The attempted Arabization of the P.C.P., despite the presumable reservations of a section of its Jewish leadership, can be noted in the basic organizational and political policies of the Palestine Communist movement since the 1930's. This shift was indicated by the transfer of the post of secretary-general to an Arab, Ridwān al-Hilū, the suspension of regular publications in Hebrew and Yiddish, and the stress on periodicals in Arabic

(manifestos and pamphlets, however, continued to appear in all three languages).[8]

4. The trend toward Arabization, accompanied by attempts to establish Arabic cadres who had been trained in the U.S.S.R., was not very successful. The P.C.P. then began to seek support among the feudal and nationalist Arab elements while continuing to brandish the slogan "For the good of the fellahin [Arab peasants] and the workers!" Open P.C.P. support for extreme Arab nationalism in Palestine reached the point of identification with the extreme nationalist religious leader, the Grand Mufti of Jerusalem, Ḥajj Amīn al-Ḥusainī, and the terrorists he organized against the British and the Jews.[9]

5. Despite these efforts, the majority of the leading cadres of the P.C.P. remained Jewish throughout the period under discussion, but employed extreme anti-Zionist slogans to attract Arab support. In effect, two separate party factions operated in the late 1930's within the P.C.P. During the latter part of the British Mandate, therefore, the P.C.P. cannot be viewed simply as one party from the standpoint of the continuity of both organization and propaganda.

The entry of the Soviet Union into the Second World War alongside the Allies permitted the P.C.P. to emerge from underground. Information and propaganda activities were expanded and clubrooms were opened. In this period, Communist militants fanned out among the Palestinian Arabs, in order to propagandize against the Axis Powers, in contrast to the nationalist leaders who identified themselves with the Axis in the War against Great Britain. However, despite these expanded activities, the changed attitude of the authorities toward the P.C.P., and the reflected prestige of the victories of the Red Army, the party did not gain any significant increase in membership among Jews or Arabs.

The turning point in the conditions surrounding Communist activity was provided by Russian support for the establishment of the State of Israel, culminating with the act of recognition in 1948.[10] Recognition of the State of Israel by the U.S.S.R. was a blow to the Communists who, ever since the foundation of their party, had combated Zionism. Even so, this shift in Russian policy did create more favorable objective conditions for Communist work in Israel. The very establishment of the State altered the conditions for Communist activity in other ways as well. In contrast to the Mandate period, the existence of a democratic parliamentary framework also made possible open, regular, and continuous political party work.[11]

In the State of Israel, MAQI regained its unity. Jews and Arabs were reunited within the organizational framework on the basis of a single common program, though the party's propaganda may not always have been at one with itself. Within the Jewish community MAQI continued to be a marginal factor, gaining temporary support from immigrants who had met with absorption difficulties. In contrast, the clear trend of MAQI's development since 1948 has been toward the fulfillment of the aim of Arabization the party had failed to achieve during the Mandate period. This process is expressed in the sharp numerical rise in the Arab communist vote. There is far-reaching disproportion in the relative support given to MAQI by Arabs as compared to Jews. Several explanations may be given for this phenomenon, among which are the following:

1. MAQI is the oldest Israeli party active among the Arabs.

2. The growing estrangement of the U.S.S.R. from the State of Israel and the increasing Soviet influence in the Arab Middle East enabled MAQI to take advantage of this situation and become the principal mouthpiece for the nationalist feelings aroused among part of the Arab population of Israel in reaction to the establishment of the State.

This growing dependence of MAQI on the Arab community emphasized its marginal status within the Jewish majority in the State.

On the political parliamentary front, the Communist Party has been and remains a small marginal party. It operates alongside four relatively large blocs that compete for 120 Knesset seats on the basis of a proportional representation system in which the whole country forms one large constituency. These blocs in order of decreasing size are: the Labor Center (MAPAI); the Right Center and the Right (Liberals and Herut); the Religious Bloc (the National Religious Party, Agudat Isra'el, and Po'alei Agudat Isra'el); and the Zionist Left (Le-Ahdut ha-'Avoda and MAPAM).[12] The Knesset seats held by each of the parties in the Fourth and Fifth Knessets are shown in the following table.[13]

TABLE 1

PARTIES IN THE FOURTH AND FIFTH KNESSETS

Party		4th K.	5th K.
		1959	1961
MAPAI		47	42
Herut		17	17
Liberals		14	17
National Religious	} Religious	12	12
Agudat Isra'el--Po'alei A. I.	} parties	6	6
MAPAM		9	9
Le-Ahdut ha-'Avoda		7	8
MAQI (Communists)		3	5
Arab minority parties		5	4
Total		120	120

Although continuously small and marginal, MAQI's
position has undergone rises and falls in popular support.
The shifts in its electoral strength and in its Knesset representation in the five general elections since the establishment of the State are summarized below.[14]

11

TABLE 2

MAQI'S KNESSET STRENGTH

	1st K.	2d K.	3d K.	4th K.	5th K.
	Jan. 1949	July 1951	July 1955	Nov. 1959	Aug. 1961
Percentage of valid votes	3.5%	4.0%	4.5%	2.8%	4.2%
Number of valid votes	15,148	27,334	38,492	27,374	42,111
Knesset seats	4	5	6	3	5

II. COMPOSITION OF THE PARTY

Structure

The structure of the Israeli Communist Party does
not differ from that of other Communist parties. The main
institutions are a Central Committee, Secretariat, Political
Bureau, and Control Committee. The ostensibly supreme
party institution--the national congress--is supposed to
meet once every three years, according to the party constitution, [15] in order to elect the central committee and the
party control committee. Between congresses, all party
institutions are subject to the central committee. In fact,
four years elapsed between the 13th and 14th Congresses;
the latter met in Tel-Aviv in June 1961. Varying periods
intervened between previous congresses: the 11th Cong-
ress--the first held after the establishment of the State of
Israel--met in 1949 while the 12th met in 1952. The links
between the cells and the regional and central institutions
are organized hierarchically, as in other Communist parties.

13

One of MAQI's noteworthy features is the wide disparity between the actual number of party members and the number of Communist votes in elections. Obviously the party does not furnish membership figures. Laqueur[16] claims that there were 5,000 members in 1955. The 1962 Annual Supplement of the Great Soviet Encyclopaedia,[17] probably referring to 1961, indicates that MAQI had 3,000 members. These figures point to the extent of organized party membership; naturally, MAQI is assisted by additional supporters and militants in front organizations and elsewhere. MAQI is a skeleton party par excellence in both the Jewish and Arab communities,[18] though not to an equal degree. This feature arises from the fact that MAQI, like other Communist parties, views itself as an elite forming the vanguard of a class. As such its ranks are open only to those who, having been found suitable, are prepared to assume the burdens and sacrifices involved. From this elitist approach also arises the status of "candidate membership." Candidates form a middle circle of activists and constitute a link between the central nucleus and the broader group of supporters. Obviously, a number of supporters

14

have no interest in becoming formal members of the party and limit themselves to financial contributions and casting their votes. The existence of this body of ''candidate members'' and supporters partially explains the disparity between the number of formal members and the number of votes won by the party in elections. The small number of formal members may also indicate the relatively greater importance of ideology as a factor leading to party membership in MAQI than in some mass Communist parties in Western Europe.

Ethnic Composition

According to a party announcement of 1961, Jews constituted 74.3 per cent of the members and Arabs 25.7 per cent.[19] At that time, however, Arabs constituted only 11 per cent of Israel's total population.

The ethnic breakdown of MAQI's membership is expressed in the composition of the directing organs of the party. Nevertheless, the shifts in the ethnic composition of the party membership are not directly reflected in the party organs whose make-up has remained fairly constant.

The last two congresses made scarcely any change in the
party organs, although there were probably marked changes
in the ethnic distribution of party membership in the eight
years covered by these congresses, as can be inferred from
MAQI's own statements at the 14th Party Congress in 1961.
The ethnic composition of the leading party institutions
elected at or after the 13th Congress (1957) and the 14th
(1961) is summarized in the following table:[20]

TABLE 3

JEWS AND ARABS IN MAQI'S PRINCIPAL INSTITUTIONS

Organs	1957		1961	
	Jews	Arabs	Jews	Arabs
Central Committee	14	6	14	5
Political Bureau	5	2	5	2

It is worth noting that the reflection of the ethnic
make-up of the party's membership in the composition of
the leading party organs strengthens the implication of the
disparity between the ethnic composition of the party's popular vote in Knesset elections and the make-up of its membership lists.

16

Composition According to
Length of Residence

Data published by MAQI indicate that 83.8 per cent

of the total membership in 1961 had joined since the estab-

lishment of the State and more than one quarter after the

beginning of 1957.[21] In other words, since the 16.2 per

cent of the 1961 membership who had been affiliated before

1948 were mostly Jews, at least 58.1 per cent were Jews

who immigrated after the establishment of the State (74.3

per cent minus 16.2 per cent). There were only small

groups of veteran settlers who joined the party after 1948,

among them several members of the Freedom Fighters of

Israel (the so-called Stern Gang), an extreme anti-British

terrorist organization. This means that among MAQI's

Jewish members, the proportion of new immigrants was

much higher than in the general population, amounting to

78.2 per cent as compared to 45.6 per cent in the total

Jewish population,[22] in 1961. Confirmation of the relative

frequency of new immigrants in Communist ranks is found

in party publications[23] listing its strength in various dis-

tricts. These reveal that the greatest increase in party

strength in 1960-1961 took place in the Negev--an area
where the party had support neither among Bedouin Arabs
(among whom the Communist vote is extremely low) nor in
Jewish kibbutzim (whose members are imbued with Zionist
ideology). This increase stemmed from the new Jewish
immigrants who have been settled in the development towns
of the Negev; for example, the secretary of MAQI's Ash-
qelon-Negev branch reported in 1961 that "almost all the
members are new immigrants."[24]

Age Composition

A large majority of the party's youthful members--
aged up to 25 years--are new adherents. According to
MAQI, this group constituted 9.2 per cent of all members
in 1961. However, in the largest Jewish urban center,
Tel-Aviv-Jaffa, this age group furnished merely 4.6 per
cent of the members as compared to almost 21 per cent in
Nazareth,[25] the largest Arab center. Thus one may assume
that the party's Arab members are on the whole younger
than the Jewish. This difference may be ascribed to the
breakdown of the traditional family structure, part of the

modernization process affecting Israeli Arabs, and the fact that the Communists have less appeal for the older, uneducated Arabs and, indeed, probably have little interest in recruiting them into the party. Among the Jews, young people are able to make an easier adjustment to the Israeli way of life than the mature adults. A large proportion of Jewish youth has been educated in Israeli Hebrew schools, has served in the armed forces of Israel, and is less attracted to MAQI. Jewish adults among the new immigrants, however, meet with certain difficulties in gaining suitable jobs and in adjusting to new patterns of life[26] and are thus more receptive to Communist propaganda than veteran settlers and young immigrants.

Composition According to Land of Origin

The 1961 Communist Party census divides the membership according to land of origin as follows:[27]

Europe	54.6%
Asia	11.4
Africa	3.1
America	1.1
Israel (Palestine)	29.8
	100.0%

19

This division deserves some comment. Firstly, if Arabs constitute, as indicated above, 25.7 per cent of all party members, all born in Palestine, then only 4.1 per cent of MAQI's Jewish members are native-born Israelis. Secondly, 55.7 per cent of MAQI's members are of European and American origin, i.e., natives of developed countries, whereas only 14.5 per cent are immigrants of African or Asian birth.

If one compares the composition of the Jewish population of the State of Israel in December 1960 and the composition of Jewish immigration in the period 1948-1960 to the aforementioned data, one finds a noticeable disproportion between the 14.5 per cent of MAQI's members from African and Asian countries and the over-all percentage of people from these areas in the Jewish population as a whole, which was 27.82 per cent or nearly double. This disproportion is even more pronounced when one considers that at least 78.2 per cent of MAQI's Jewish members are new immigrants and 52.34 per cent of the Jewish immigrants to Israel in the period 1948-1960 were from Asia and Africa. Similarly, the percentage of Jewish members of MAQI from

Europe and America (55.7 per cent of the whole) is far larger than this group's share of the total Jewish population, which was 35.13 per cent on December 31, 1960, and larger than its percentage among all immigrants to Israel during 1948-1960, namely 45.66 per cent.[28]

These divergencies may be explained by the fact that a large proportion of the African and Asian immigrants had lived under patriarchal-feudal conditions, respected authority, and had little predisposition to join extreme opposition parties like MAQI. In addition, a large proportion are no worse off, and often far better off, than in their lands of origin. Certainly the majority of these immigrants have no reason to join MAQI as a form of economic protest.

A majority of Jewish immigrants from Europe and America, however, lacks this ingrained respect for authority; even those coming from the "People's Republics" have not lived there long enough to be fully conditioned to identify themselves with the regime. Accustomed to a comfortable life in their lands of origin, some had difficulty in adjusting to Israeli life and expressed their discontent by joining an opposition party, largely as a form of economic protest.[29]

This phenomenon was especially common among those who had been members of, or activists in, Communist parties in Eastern Europe.

Educational and Occupational Composition

The data regarding the educational and occupational background of MAQI members derived from the party census of 1960-1961 are not very helpful.[30] Worthy of note is the low percentage, 3.2 per cent, of illiterates in the party, as compared to 16.9 per cent and 55.7 per cent for Jews and Arabs, respectively, in the population as a whole in 1959.[31] This disproportion may be explained on the grounds that those who lack education tend to shy away from active party membership; it may also be that the relatively high illiteracy rate among Israeli Arabs is also reflected among MAQI members.

MAQI made only one distinction in its census regarding occupation--that existing between wage-earners and self-employed. The latter term, however, contains so wide a variety of categories--liberal professions, shopkeepers, and farmers--that its meaning is blurred. It should be

22

noted that the country-wide percentage of wage-earners of

all types (this figure is not affected to the same degree by

the failure to distinguish between categories) is 78 per cent

of all gainfully employed members of the party (as compared

to 22 per cent self-employed). According to this source,

the percentage of housewives is 7.1 per cent. MAQI claims

that 24.6 per cent of its members in 1961 were women and

17.5 per cent of the total were working women.[32] Thus,

almost one third of the female members of the party were

housewives, a not insignificant proportion for a party which

addresses itself to workers.

The Leadership

The central organs of the party are made up of mili-

tants, the majority of whom are paid members of the party

staff. A number of these, particularly the Arabs, are new

members who joined after the establishment of the State.

The leadership is concentrated, however, in an inner circle

of Jews and Arabs who repeatedly share the most important

party positions. Most prominent are the Jews: Shmu'el

Miqunis, born in 1903, the Secretary General of the party

and a member of all the central party institutions; Me'īr
Vīlner, born in 1918, the Chairman of the Secretariat of
MAQI and a member of the Central Committee and the Political Bureau; Esther Vīlensqa, born in 1918, a member of
the Central Committee and the Political Bureau; Moshe
Sneh, born in 1909, a member of the Central Committee
and the Political Bureau; Zvī Breitstein, husband of Esther
Vīlensqa, Chairman of the Control Committee and an editor
of Qōl ha-'am, the party's Hebrew daily. Also prominent
are the Arabs, Emil Ḥabībī and Taufīq Ṭūbī, both born in
1922, who are also members of the party's central organs.
The party's representatives in the Knesset are also drawn
from this group.

Not much is known about the personalities of the
party's important leaders. They are publicity shy, and few
details concerning them or their past are reported in the
press. The Great Soviet Encyclopaedia mentions only
Mīqūnis[33] in a very brief article. The above-mentioned
Jewish leaders were all born in Eastern Europe and immigrated to Palestine between the two World Wars.[34] All of
them belong to the intelligentsia, and few, if any, have

24

been manual laborers.[35] Habībī[36] and Ṭūbī, both born in Haifa,[37] represent the Palestinian Arabs and are intellectuals who have never done manual work;[38] they are veteran Communists, remnants of the pre-1948 leadership of the party.

MAQI's top leadership is made up of a small number of veterans who have been active since the period of the British Mandate, and who have led the party at least since the establishment of the State of Israel. This leadership--particularly Shmū'el Mīqūnīs, who has held the key post of Secretary General--has managed to maintain its position continuously. It has not been shaken by the convulsions in the Communist world since the end of the Second World War. Paradoxically, these leaders are noted for their stubborn dogmatism, reflected as recently as 1962 by the adoption of a pro-Chinese attitude in the Sino-Indian crisis, before a volte-face was performed and the party finally aligned itself with Moscow. Despite active journalistic and propaganda work, no theoretical political or economic studies have yet been published. The only one with pretenses as a theorist is Moshe Sneh, who joined the Communists rather later than

25

the others after a political career in the bourgeois Zionist parties. This was apparently the outcome of Sneh's feeling, after the end of the Second World War, that a Jewish State could be founded through Russian support only.

The 26 Jews in the central institutions of the party constitute a very heterogeneous group as regards their social origin, educational background, and the factors which led them to MAQI. Eastern Europe predominates among their lands of origin, and there is practically no representation from among the Oriental Jewish communities. The latter is surprising, inasmuch as ''integration of the exiles'' occupies an important place among the political issues in the State, and MAQI has taken a clear stand against what it terms discrimination against the Oriental Jewish communities.

III. MAJOR POLITICAL POSITIONS
AND MEANS OF PROPAGANDA

Conflicting Positions toward Israel

Just as MAQI's composition differs from that of
some other Communist parties, so one can distinguish special differences with regard to its political positions. Two
fundamental contrasts are visible in MAQI's political propaganda since the establishment of the State of Israel in 1948.

At certain times during the British Mandate in Palestine, the P.C.P. found it easy to call on both Jews and
Arabs to oppose the British regime.[39] After the State was
established and subsequent to the short period of warm
Soviet support for Israel, however, a fundamental change
occurred in the content of the Communist Party's propaganda. MAQI has firmly rejected Jewish nationalism, i.e.,
Zionism. It has opposed promotion of links between the
State and the Jewish people in the Diaspora and the encouragement of Jewish migration to Israel. At the same time,
MAQI has declared itself an enthusiastic supporter of, and

27

loyal spokesman for, the national aims of the Israeli Arabs.
This contradiction in its attitude toward the national aims of
the Jews and the Arabs provides the first of the above-mentioned contrasts.

The second contrast stems from the Communist
position regarding the very existence of the State of Israel.
MAQI does not dispute the raison d'être of the State and
accepts Israel's existence alongside all other states.[40]
Nevertheless, MAQI denies the validity of and opposes the
Zionist ideal that was the motive for the creation of the
Jewish National Home in Palestine and its transformation
into a State and that continues to hold a central place in the
Israeli consensus and in public policy. If the Jews of Palestine had the right to bring their Zionism to the stage of
fulfillment by establishing the State, as agreed to by MAQI
a posteriori, it seems rather inconsistent of the Communists to continue to fight the Zionist ideal.

These contrasts are the source of MAQI's variations
in its approach to the Jewish and Arab communities, which
are expressed in detail in the party's Knesset election propaganda. The emphasis in its propaganda is different among

Jews and Arabs, but both campaigns are nourished from the same ideological line. This is confirmed in the summaries of party congresses which are brought to the attention of the public, in MAQI's programs in Hebrew and Arabic, and in the ad-hoc resolutions passed by the central institutions of the party.

Despite differences in approach to Arabs and Jews, imposed by issues of the day or made necessary by tactical maneuvers, MAQI has not varied its programs and propaganda since the establishment of the State in its appeals on questions of major policy, both in Hebrew and in Arabic. Major policy lines have been determined, firstly, to accord with the general policies of the Soviet Union in the Middle East, and, secondly, by MAQI's relative popular strength in the two Israeli sectors. These major policies may be summarized as follows.

Israel-Arab Relations

On the central question of Israel-Arab relations, MAQI no longer advocates the foundation of an Arab state in Palestine, as it did in the early years of the State of

Israel. It demands, however, that peace in the area be fostered via territorial concessions by Israel and a return of the Arab refugees.[41] Here MAQI on the one hand consistently ignores the stand of the Arab states on the question of peace with Israel, and on the other hand stresses what it terms the intransigence of Israel. The fact that the question of peace with the Arabs remains first on Israel's political agenda provides fertile ground for MAQI's propaganda.

Foreign Policy

In the field of foreign policy, political and economic, MAQI demands that the State of Israel "give up its pro-Western orientation and adopt positive neutrality toward the Eastern bloc," and that Israel break its ties with West Germany and in any event denounce what MAQI terms the militarism of a government in which ex-Nazis hold important positions. In the field of foreign economic relations, the party demands that Israel be liberated from foreign capital--principally American. In the early years of the State, MAQI opposed American loans (attached to which it discovered "militarist strings," particularly during the

Korean War). It opposed Western capital investments in 1961 as imposing economic enslavement, and in unison with the Soviet Union it denounced the Common Market along with Israel's attempts to forge links with the latter.

The Social and Economic System

On social and economic questions MAQI shares the well-known views of Communist parties with their stress on the class war. Its tone is a function of its feeling of strength or show of force, shifting from a demand for "the overthrow of the capitalist slave system"[42] (in 1951, the peak year of Stalin's aggressiveness) to a demand for "the leadership of the working class guided by the Communist Party"[43] (in 1955, after MAQI's relative success in elections to the General Federation of Labor--Histadrut). More recently, MAQI has sounded the more modest note of "social reforms for the benefit of the toilers, through satisfying demands for the welfare of all the workers, raising real wages at the expense of company profits, reducing taxes, and abolishing social polarization"[44] (1961).

Relations with Minorities

In the field of minority relations, MAQI demands removal of controls over the freedom of movement of Arabs living in border areas[45] as well as the abolition of other limitations imposed by the Military Administration.

Propaganda Means

MAQI conducts its propaganda directly or through front organizations and cooperating groups such as the Organization of Anti-Nazi Fighters, the Women's Democratic Union, the Israel-Soviet Union Friendship Movement, and similar organizations for the development of friendly relations with Poland, Rumania, Czechoslovakia, and more recently Communist China. Another platform is provided by the Young Communist League (known as BANQI). The friendship organizations appeal principally to Jewish immigrants from the countries mentioned. The party makes use of the publications, manifestos, and meetings of these organizations for its propaganda; the latter in turn use the party's permanent clubrooms.

MAQI periodicals appear in Hebrew or Arabic (or other languages), but its only daily newspaper is published in Hebrew. The journalistic standard of Qōl ha-'am is as high as that of many other daily Hebrew newspapers, but circulation is apparently limited to Jewish party members and supporters. The Hebrew periodical Ba-Derekh (On the Road) deals mainly with ideological matters and contains much material translated from other languages.

The Arabic fortnightly al-Ittiḥad (The Union) is of as high a standard, at least, as other Arabic-language newspapers in Israel; its pages contain not only reports of current events but the literary works of several of the best Arabic writers in Israel. The Arabic periodical al-Darb (The Road) follows the policy of the Hebrew Ba-Derekh. The Arabic monthly al-Jadīd (The New) is of a purely literary nature, emphasizing social questions. Another Arabic monthly, al-Ghad (Tomorrow), addresses itself to youth.[46]

To these one should add periodicals in various languages intended for Jewish immigrants from Europe. Six of these deserve mention (the first five are weeklies and the last is a monthly): La Voix du Peuple (French: Voice of the People); Glasul Poporului (Rumanian: Voice of the

People); Népszava (Hungarian: Voice of the People);

Naroden Glas (Bulgarian: Popular Voice); Frei Yisroel

(Yiddish: Free Israel); and Walka (Polish: Struggle).[47]

Other propaganda materials include pamphlets and

various manifestos, published in the main before elections;

of these one must mention Hebrew pamphlets that include

the reports of party congresses.

IV. ORGANIZATION AND PROPAGANDA
ON THE EVE OF THE 1961 ELECTIONS

MAQI was assisted in preparing for the Fifth Knesset elections of 1961 by far more favorable conditions than those prevalent in 1959. Its best previous record in popular votes and Knesset seats was achieved in 1955 (Third Knesset). The Twentieth Congress of the Communist Party of the Soviet Union, the changes in Poland, and the Hungarian uprising of 1956 caused many to turn their backs on the party, which suffered a sharp drop in popular support and seats in the 1959 elections (Fourth Knesset). Less than two years later, however, MAQI was able to capitalize on the increased scientific prestige of the Soviet Union and the impact of the new program of the C.P.S.U. on those susceptible to Communist ideology, to restore the position lost in 1959.

In 1961, MAQI left no stone unturned in its efforts to gain votes. It paid unprecedented attention to broadening its organizational framework among both Jews and Arabs.

New branches were established in immigrant areas; party activists and propaganda penetrated into every possible place that appeared open to them. A special fund-raising drive among members and supporters of the party[48] on the eve of MAQI's 14th Congress, scheduled a mere month and a half before the Knesset elections, alerted the militants and prepared the party for the election campaign.

The party's 14th Congress saw no major shifts in the party line, but it had great organization and propaganda value. Me'ïr Vïlner's report to the Congress on party membership[49] analyzed and indicated where expansion was possible. Rallies in various localities, with the participation of foreign visitors who had come especially for the Congress, raised MAQI's prestige and served as an effective send-off for the election campaign. Subsequent activity included meetings, canvassing in particular localities, and publications in Hebrew, Arabic, and some languages commonly used by the new Jewish immigrants. This propaganda, naturally, stressed the principal themes of the major policies outlined above, along with descriptions of the Soviet successes in the conquest of space during the summer of

1961, as well as extracts from the new program of the C.P.S.U. Other subjects included may be divided into three groups.

Subjects Stressed for Jews

Three facts were emphasized in the propaganda aimed at the Jews: (1) the Eichmann trial, (2) wage increases, and (3) identification with new immigrants.

1. The Eichmann trial, whose conclusion coincided with the Fifth Knesset election campaign, provided the Communists with an opportunity to seek the support of the victims of the Nazis and their families by criticizing Israel's relations with West Germany.

2. MAQI took advantage of the pressure for wage increases by skilled workers and the working intelligentsia, in reaction to the rise in prices of various commodities (as a matter of fact, this pressure should be viewed against the background of full employment and the shortage of skilled workers which made it possible to exploit the approaching elections in order to extract wage concessions from the government and employers in the private and public sectors).

The party voiced support for the workers in every industry
and branch who demanded wage increases and who threatened or were conducting strikes; even Rabbis who were
State employees won MAQI's attention when they were con-
sidering strike action![50] The party supported a struggle
against the General Federation of Labor, local labor councils, and employers--launched by unofficial workers'
"action committees." Also worthy of special mention is
MAQI's identification with underprivileged groups of workers to the extent of backing individuals among the unskilled.
During this period, a full page, every day, in Qol ha-'am
described actual and threatened strikes, many of which
never materialized.

3. This identification with groups of discontented
workers was similar in tendency to MAQI's appeal to groups
of new immigrants who were still meeting difficulties in
adjusting to a new society. The Communists were especially active in organizing meetings among concentrations
of immigrants who had not yet received permanent quarters,
as well as in slum areas with poor sanitary and municipal
services. MAQI also attempted to appear the champion of

Oriental communities in an effort to prove that these were suffering from bias. The content of MAQI propaganda and the large number of meetings held in immigrant neighborhoods in large cities indicate that the Communists made little effort to win the veteran, settled Jewish population. They paid scant attention to the central issues that aroused the interest of this population in 1961, such as the "Lavon Affair" and the position of the Histadrut in the State.

Subjects Stressed for Arabs

Three broad trends were highlighted in party propaganda directed at the Arabs: (1) nationalism, (2) equality, and (3) socioeconomic benefits.

1. MAQI tried to present itself as the sole non-Zionist party in Israel and thus as the sole defender of the Arab national interest in the State.

2. The Communists also attempted to pose as the only consistent fighters for the abolition of the Military Administration and as opponents of attempts to expropriate Arab lands for security purposes or national irrigation works. The struggle of the Moslems to elect their own

qādis (religious judges)[51] and the Druze struggle for religious autonomy[52] received the full support of the Communists.

3. Faced with a substantial rise in the over-all standard of living, the Communists paid special attention to those sectors of Arab society within which there existed fringes of discontent--notably among the few unemployed peasants and workers. MAQI ably addressed itself to the whole Arab community on nationalist and equalitarian grounds and to peasants and workers on economic grounds. It also stressed local grievances, attempting to exploit the needs of large and small localities in the areas of health, sanitation, road-mending, water supply, and the establishment and upkeep of schools.

Subjects Stressed for Both Jews and Arabs

Many of the subjects stressed for one of the two communities were also brought to the attention of the other, but to a different extent and with a different emphasis. In addition to the major policy lines, there were a number of special issues on which MAQI appealed to both communities.

MAQI revealed a desire to identify itself with the aspirations of both the Jewish and the Arab intelligentsia, particularly the salaried intelligentsia. The goal of drawing Arab women into the Communist fold coincided with the party's concern for the problems of working women in the Jewish community. In both of these sectors the Communists operated systematically and continuously within every dissatisfied group on every level.

41

V. THE ELECTIONS OF AUGUST 15, 1961

The Total Communist Vote

On August 15, 1961, a total of 1,037,030 voters, or
81.6 per cent of the electorate, cast 1,006,964 valid ballots.
MAQI received 42,111 or 4.18 per cent of the valid votes,
14,737 more than in 1959 (see Table 2).[53] This was a rise
of 54 per cent in comparison with the 1959 Fourth Knesset
elections and a larger vote than in the 1955 Third Knesset
elections in absolute terms; nevertheless, the 1961 percentage of valid votes was slightly lower than the 4.51 per cent
obtained in 1955.

Monoethnic Arab and Jewish localities and polyethnic
or mixed cities should be distinguished in the detailed analysis of MAQI's election results in order to establish its following in the Arab and Jewish communities respectively.
This distinction is justified because the Communist vote in
purely Arab localities differs from that in the Jewish or
mixed areas. It is not difficult to make this distinction in
purely Arab or Jewish localities, but no differentiation along

42

ethnic lines is made in mixed cities in the counting of ballots
or the publication of results. Nevertheless, the concentration of most of the Arab population in particular neighborhoods of the mixed cities helps clarify the relative weight of
the Arab vote in these areas.

The Communist Vote in
Purely Arab Localities

In purely Arab localities, 87 per cent of the 92, 125
eligible voters (7.8 per cent of the total in the country) cast
76, 918 valid ballots. Since MAQI received about 17, 000 of
these votes, [54] i.e., slightly more than 22 per cent, its
vote in purely Arab areas was five times greater than its
country-wide average and far above its percentage in purely
Jewish areas. In the 1959 Knesset elections, MAQI had
obtained only 11 per cent of the votes in purely Arab localities, and this had accounted for merely 29 per cent of the
Communist vote. [55] In 1961, however, 40 per cent of all
Communist votes came from these areas, which represent
only 7.7 per cent of the total votes.

43

TABLE 4

COMMUNIST VOTES BY ETHNIC COMMUNITY IN 1959 AND 1961

Ethnic Area	Percentage of Valid Votes in Area, Based on Country-wide Total		MAQI's Percentage of Votes in the Area		Percentage of MAQI's Country-wide Vote Received in the Area	
	1959	1961	1959	1961	1959	1961
Purely Arab localities	7.4	7.7	11.00	22.00	29.58	40.39
Purely Jewish and mixed localities	92.6	92.3	2.15	2.67	70.42	59.61
	100.0	100.0			100.00	100.00

The Communist vote in Arab localities was not evenly distributed. Out of the 140 Arab localities of all sizes in which polling stations were established, one can isolate 35 settlements[56] with 46,389 votes (60.2 per cent of the valid ballots in purely Arab areas), which yielded 91 per cent or 15,471 out of the 17,000 votes MAQI won in purely Arab areas. It thus appears that only some 1,500 Communist votes were cast in the other 105 purely Arab localities (or three-quarters of the 140) with a total of 30,000 votes. In these 105 localities, MAQI's percentage did not rise above 5 per cent as compared to an average of 33.3 per cent in the 35 localities mentioned above.

The 35 purely Arab localities with a high percentage of Communist votes are scattered about Galilee and the "Little Triangle"[57] and are populated by Moslems, Druzes, and Christians of various denominations. Because of their multi-religious character, there is no possibility of analyzing the vote in these localities according to religious groups. Nevertheless, it is possible to divide the Communist vote of these 35 localities into four groups based on population size.

TABLE 5

1961 COMMUNIST VOTES IN 35 PURELY ARAB LOCALITIES
BY POPULATION SIZE

Size of Locality (Total Number of Valid Votes)	Number of Localities	Total Number of Valid Votes Cast	MAQI's Total Number of Votes	MAQI's Percentage of Valid Votes
Over 2,600	1 (Nazareth)	9,239	4,278	46.3
1,600-2,600	7	15,603	5,008	32.1
800-1,600	12	13,166	4,028	30.6
150-800	15	8,381	2,157	25.7
T o t a l	35	46,389	15,471	33.3
Other Arab localities	105	30,000 (approx.)	1,500 (approx.)	5.0

46

This comparison of the above-mentioned 35 purely Arab localities with a high percentage of Communist votes in the 1961 Knesset elections reveals a tendency to regularity--namely, the larger the population (the number of votes) the higher the percentage of Communist votes.

It is noteworthy that in the 1959 Fourth Knesset elections as well, the Communist vote in these localities was higher than in the other purely Arab settlements and displayed the same regularity. The 1959 vote is shown in Table 6.

A comparison of Tables 5 and 6 also indicates that the large increase in Communist votes in 1961 was derived mainly from purely Arab localities. Out of the national increase of 14,737 Communist votes in 1961 as compared to 1959, the sum of 8,904 votes (or 60.3 per cent of the increase) came from purely Arab localities, with the 35 localities mentioned above providing 8,078 of these additional votes or 90.7 per cent of the increase in purely Arab localities.

MAQI's additional votes in these 35 places varied between 14.8 per cent and 18.1 per cent of the votes cast

47

TABLE 6

1959 COMMUNIST VOTES IN 35 PURELY ARAB LOCALITIES
BY POPULATION SIZE

Size of Locality (Total Number of Valid Votes)	Number of Localities	Total Number of Valid Votes Cast	MAQI's Total Number of Votes	MAQI's Percentage of Valid Votes
Over 2,600	1 (Nazareth)	8,495	2,397	28.2
1,600-2,600	7	14,285	2,285	16.0
800-1,600	12	12,407	1,956	15.8
150-800	15	8,317	755	9.1
Total	35	43,504	7,393	16.9
Other Arab localities	105	28,216	703	1.6

there. This increase, although fairly uniform, conformed in the larger localities with the tendency noted above, namely, the direct relationship between Communist votes and population size. Only in the smaller localities (150-180 votes) was there a slight upward deviation from this regularity. There was, however, a significant difference between the 35 localities mentioned above and the other purely Arab localities where the percentage increase was much lower (as shown in Table 7).

Three features stand out in the distribution of Communist votes among purely Arab localities: (1) the great disparity between MAQI's vote in the 35 places selected and the other 105; (2) the relation between population size and the strength of the Communist vote--a relation that coincides to a great extent with the more sizable increase in the larger as compared to the medium and smaller localities; and (3) the fact that, without affecting the order of the absolute size of the Communist vote among groups of localities ranked according to the number of voters, MAQI's relative gains (i.e., the increase, in 1961, in terms of the percentage obtained in 1959) were greater in the smaller localities.

TABLE 7

THE 1959-1961 INCREASE IN COMMUNIST VOTES
IN PURELY ARAB LOCALITIES

Size of Locality (Total Number of Valid Votes)	Number of Localities	MAQI's Percentage of Valid Votes		Increase in MAQI's Vote (Percentage of Valid Votes)
		1959	1961	
Over 2,600	1 (Nazareth)	28.2	46.3	18.1
1,600-2,600	7	16.0	32.1	16.1
800-1,600	12	15.8	30.6	14.8
150-800	15	9.1	25.7	16.6
Other Arab localities	105	1.6	5.0	3.4

Thus, while MAQI doubled its relative strength in purely
Arab localities (from 11 per cent in 1959 to 22 per cent in
1961), its relative growth in Nazareth was merely 60 per
cent compared to a threefold growth in the small localities.

Various characteristic factors contributed to these
tendencies: (1) Communist propaganda and election meetings were concentrated in the 35 places selected; practically
no MAQI election meetings were reported in any other Arab
locality; (2) the more populous an area and the more fre-
quent and varied the forms of social communication (and
apparently the higher the literacy rate), the more appropriate the background and the broader the social base for positive receptivity to extremist political propaganda; and (3)
even in the less populous Arab centers, where Communist
strength was smaller than in the larger localities, a certain
weakening of the traditional family framework has occurred.
A relevant feature is supplied by landless Arab youths,
whom the villages cannot support and who therefore seek
work in the cities.[58] (The number of young people has
grown more than proportionally with the great increase in
the over-all size of the Arab population of the State, from

120,000 in 1948 to 250,000 in 1961.) Most of these people, although working in the towns, vote in their own villages. These voters have grown accustomed to the freedom of the secret ballot and have used it, even in small places, to vote in relatively larger numbers for an extreme opposition party.

When one compares MAQI's growth in the 1961 election to the fate of other parties in purely Arab centers, the following facts may be discerned. Firstly, two constant features appear in each locality almost without exception-- the rise of MAQI and the complementary decline, and sometimes even the complete failure, of the independent Arab lists (two Arab lists that were not allied with any Jewish party and were led by Arab leaders who had abandoned their alliance with MAPAI). Secondly, from an over-all viewpoint, there was a decline in support, within purely Arab areas, for MAPAI and its allied Arab lists. Thirdly, the same was true for MAPAM in the 1961 elections.[59] With regard to MAPAI and its allied lists, the rate of decline increased as the group of localities grew smaller; whereas for MAPAM, the decline was greatest in the larger centers

52

with little change in smaller places (where its vote even rose to a minor degree). These were, however, general tendencies, and deviations can be detected in each category of localities.

Among the parties operating systematically and continuously in the Arab sector, only MAQI can be said to have grown significantly while the other three groups of parties-- MAPAI and its allied Arab lists, MAPAM, and the independent Arab lists--declined, thus nourishing the Communist rise (see Table 8).

Notwithstanding the drop in support for MAPAI and its allied lists, it should be borne in mind that they still have the largest percentage of votes in purely Arab localities. This is interesting inasmuch as MAQI directed its main attack against MAPAI, but Communist gains have been made largely at the expense of the independent Arab lists. Those who support MAPAI and its allies apparently recognize the contributions of the government, headed by MAPAI, to the rise in the Arab standard of living and the modernization of villages and towns; support for the dominant party is also natural for a community whose development depends

53

TABLE 8

DISTRIBUTION OF VOTES IN 1959 AND 1961 FOR PRINCIPAL PARTIES IN 35 SELECTED ARAB LOCALITIES

Localities	Year	MAQI (%)	MAPAI and Allied Arab Lists (%)	Independent Arab Lists (%)	MAPAM (%)
Over 2,600	1959	28.2	37.2	12.3	13.4
Valid votes (Nazareth)	1961	46.3 +18.1	37.1 - 0.1	1.1 -11.2	9.9 - 3.5
1,600-2,600	1959	16.0	44.0	12.1	10.8
Valid votes (7 localities)	1961	32.1 +16.1	43.9 - 0.1	5.8 - 6.3	7.1 - 3.7
800-1,600	1959	15.8	49.2	8.9	8.9
Valid votes (12 localities)	1961	30.6 +14.8	46.1 - 3.1	3.7 - 5.2	7.6 - 1.3
150-800	1959	9.1	54.1	11.2	11.8
Valid votes (15 localities)	1961	25.7 +16.6	46.1 - 8.0	4.8 - 6.4	12.4 + 0.6

largely on services and aid from the State authorities. On the other hand, the decline of the independent Arab lists testifies to the disappointment of many Israeli Arabs with these lists (which failed to elect even one member to the Knesset in 1959); Arab voters apparently preferred to transfer their protest votes to the Communists. As the Communist vote rose, that of MAPAM declined in all but the smaller villages; nevertheless, it won many Arab votes because of its concern for the Arab intelligentsia and the employment of Arabs in its kibbutzim. MAPAM's decline in the Arab sector may be explained by its partnership in the Government Coalition from 1955 to 1961, thus leading a section of the Arab electorate to stop viewing it as an appropriate instrument of protest.

Other Jewish parties were also active in the Arab community. Among these, the greatest effort was exerted by Le-Aḥdut ha-'Avōda (a socialist party between MAPAI and MAPAM). However, in contrast to MAQI, MAPAI, and MAPAM, all these parties operated only sporadically within the Arab community, mainly in the months immediately before the Knesset elections. Their fate varied with the

locality; in general there was little direct connection
between the shifts in the votes they obtained and the rise
in Communist strength.

The Arab Communist Vote
in Mixed Localities

Six cities whose population is largely Jewish had a
total of 13,290 eligible Arab voters in 1961. The Arabs
constitute a tiny minority of the population in these cities;
most of them are concentrated in distinct quarters, but a
scattering live in other sections of these cities, and some
Jews reside within the Arab quarters as well.[60]

Although no distinction is made between Jewish and
Arab votes in the counting and publication of election results,
an attempt will be made to isolate the Arab vote in these
mixed areas, so that shifts in MAQI's strength can be analyzed. The Jewish vote in the mixed cities varies little
from that in purely Jewish localities and will be discussed
in the section devoted to the Jewish vote.

The shifts in the Arab Communist vote between 1959
and 1961 in mixed cities are summarized in the following
table.

TABLE 9

COMPOSITION OF THE ELECTORATE IN SIX MIXED CITIES
AND THE COMMUNIST VOTE

City	Total Number of Eligible Voters	Arabs Number	Arabs %	MAQI's Percentage of All Valid Votes 1959	MAQI's Percentage of All Valid Votes 1961	MAQI's Increase (Percentage)
Tel-Aviv-Jaffa	269,762	2,974	1.10	2.7	3.3	0.6
Haifa	125,291	4,828	3.85	2.6	3.9	1.3
Jerusalem	97,926	896	0.91	1.1	1.4	0.3
Acre	12,561	2,827	22.50	4.9	11.1	6.2
Ramlah	12,422	1,101	8.86	9.2	11.5	2.3
Lydda	10,767	664	6.16	4.4	5.5	1.1

In the six mixed cities, the 13,290 Arabs constitute 2.51 per cent of the eligible voters. But there is a vast difference between Ramlah and Acre on the one hand and Jerusalem and Tel-Aviv on the other. Obviously, in the latter the Arabs cannot exercise a significant influence on the size of the Communist vote. The variations in the relative weight of the Arab vote in each of the mixed cities require individual discussion. Although the Arab votes in these cities cannot be identified, one can prove that even in these urban centers--within a Jewish milieu and atmosphere-- there is an increased tendency among the Arabs to support the Communist Party. In any case, the Arab Communist vote in the mixed cities was considerably higher than that of the Jews.

1. <u>Tel-Aviv - Jaffa</u>. Communist support in this city was 3.3 per cent of the total vote; but in the 12 polling stations where the majority of Arabs were concentrated MAQI received 13.7 per cent of the valid ballots cast.

2. <u>Haifa</u>. In the 21 polling stations used by the major segment of the Arab community, the Communists received 16.6 per cent of the votes cast. In certain areas

where the Arab concentration is probably highest, the Communist vote reached as high as 37.3, 39.8, or even 42.1 per cent of the total vote, thus approaching the figure of 46.3 per cent achieved in Nazareth, the largest all-Arab city. The 21 polling stations used by the majority of the Arab voters in Haifa provided 69.7 per cent (841 votes) of the general increase (1,206 votes) in MAQI's vote in the city as compared with 1959, although these stations provide only 11.4 per cent of the total vote and the Arab population in Haifa constitutes a mere 3.85 per cent of the total number of eligible voters. These stations also supplied almost a half (48.03 per cent) of the total Communist vote in Haifa, but only slightly more than 10 per cent of all votes in the city.

3. Acre. In Acre, where the Arabs constitute 22.5 per cent of the total number of eligible voters, their influence on MAQI's election success was even more obvious. Here, indeed, the rise in Communist votes was steeper than in any other mixed city. In the six polling stations used by almost all the Arab voters but providing only 42.9 per cent of all ballots in Acre, MAQI received 88.66 per cent of its vote. These were not Arab votes alone, but it is

significant that in the remaining polling stations, where the voters were almost exclusively Jews, MAQI received merely 11.3 per cent of its vote in Acre. In four out of the six stations with a majority of Arab voters, the Communists won 24.9, 29.8, 35.3, and 36.4 per cent of the votes.

4. Ramlah. In Ramlah 45.22 per cent of MAQI's votes were received in only five polling stations with 22.9 per cent of all valid ballots. These stations were used by the majority of Arab voters; in them the Communists received an average of 22.7 per cent of the votes cast. MAQI received only 54.8 per cent of its votes in the stations where Jews alone voted, which contained 77.1 per cent of the votes in the city.

5. Lydda. The majority of the Arab vote was concentrated in four polling stations, where 20.1 per cent of all votes were cast in 1961. Here MAQI received 43.6 per cent of its vote in Lydda. The average Communist vote in these stations was 11.8 per cent as compared to 5.5 per cent in the city as a whole.

6. Jerusalem. Here, too, where the number of both Arab and Communist votes was relatively low, one can

indicate a rise in the five polling stations where the majority of Arab voters was concentrated. MAQI received 11.31
per cent of its city-wide vote in stations containing 3.14 per
cent of the total number of votes in the city. The average
Communist vote in these five stations was 5 per cent as
compared to 1.4 per cent for Jerusalem as a whole.

The picture demonstrated by Table 10 emerges from
an examination of the Communist vote in 1961 in those polling stations in the mixed cities where the majority of Arabs
was concentrated, as compared to 1959.

The data in the table show clearly that MAQI
received its lowest vote in Jerusalem where there was practically no significant shift in the voting pattern of "Arab"
polling stations. Contrasting with this, far-reaching
changes occurred in the size of the Communist vote in the
"Arab" polling stations in Acre, Lydda, and Haifa. In
Haifa and Lydda the relative support for MAQI doubled in
"Arab" polling stations, while in Acre it rose two and a
half times. In Tel-Aviv and Ramlah the increase was by a
mere one-third. The variations in the shifts of the vote in
"Arab" polling stations in the six mixed cities indicate that

61

TABLE 10

SHIFTS IN THE COMMUNIST VOTE IN 1959-1961
IN SIX MIXED CITIES, IN MAINLY
ARAB POLLING STATIONS

City	Percentage of Communist Votes in "Arab" Polling Stations		Percentage of Total Communist Vote in City Gained in "Arab" Polling Stations	
	1959	1961	1959	1961
Tel-Aviv - Jaffa	10.06	13.70	10.68	12.67
Haifa	8.21	16.60	37.35	48.03
Jerusalem	4.60	5.10	12.07	11.31
Acre	8.95	22.91	80.89	88.66
Ramlah	17.53	22.68	44.82	45.22
Lydda	5.58	11.88	20.05	43.64

while Ramlah provided relatively the greatest support for
MAQI in 1959, Acre assumed the lead in 1961.

One reason for these variations is to be found in the
fact that Acre, Ramlah, and Lydda have the highest Arab
populations in relative terms. These concentrations facili-
tate propaganda efforts and increase the sense of security
of the more compact Arab population, as indicated by the
readiness to vote for a party that radically opposes the
established regime. The motive of economic protest car-
ries but little weight in the mixed cities where the Arabs
are fairly prosperous; hence, the principal motive for Arab
support of MAQI should be sought in nationalist sentiment.

The Patterns of the Jewish Communist Vote

In contrast to the Israeli Arab community, there
has been internal migration in the Jewish population. This
includes movement from one settlement to another, primarily from newer immigrant areas to the older established
settlements and shifts from one quarter to another within
the same locality, especially in older urban centers. This
mobility derives in part from the nature of the Jewish

population, more than half of which is composed of immigrants who arrived in Israel after 1948. Generally, immigrants display a higher rate of mobility than others. Moreover, the constant rise in the standard of living has stimulated movements of the Jewish population to what are considered preferred areas. The steady expansion of towns and villages also brings about internal population movements. Any investigator of voting patterns over a long period must bear in mind these processes, in evaluating data based on results in polling stations and localities. The mere 21 months between the Fourth and Fifth Knesset elections and the relative stability of the Jewish voting pattern, however, permit one to assume that population shifts were not significant enough to preclude evaluation of the data assembled here.

Three types of localities should be distinguished in analyzing the Jewish vote: purely Jewish agricultural settlements; mixed urban centers, where the population is predominantly Jewish; and purely Jewish centers.

Of the total votes, 131,422 or 13.05 per cent were cast in purely Jewish agricultural settlements, 406,005 or

40.32 per cent in purely Jewish urban areas, and 392,619

or 38.99 per cent in mixed urban areas. Table 11 gives the

percentage of the vote for the Communists in each category.

TABLE 11

1959-1961 SHIFTS IN THE JEWISH COMMUNIST VOTE,
BY TYPE OF LOCALITY

Type of Locality	1959	1961
Villages	0.58%	0.54%
Urban:		
Six mixed cities*	2.08%	2.29%
Purely Jewish cities	2.23%	2.49%
All urban localities (pure and mixed)	2.15%	2.39%

General average of Jewish
  Communist vote in villages
  and urban localities
	1.89%	2.13%

*Estimate.

In analyzing and explaining the over-all Jewish Com-

munist vote in 1961, one should indicate a certain parallel-

ism between the Jewish and Arab votes that reduces the

65

Communist vote in small village settlements. There is a
wide divergence between the Communist vote--Jewish and
Arab--in the villages and in urban centers, although for
different reasons, particular to each of the two communities.

The 1961 elections saw significant Communist gains
among Arabs in cities and large towns. In purely Jewish
and mixed cities, however, the increase was very slight
and the established Jewish Communist voting pattern was
maintained.

Purely Jewish Villages

In 1961 MAQI's vote was lowest in these areas; it
obtained only 713 ballots or 0.54 per cent of the votes cast
in Jewish villages. This failure was also apparent in previous Knesset elections (in 1959, 0.58 per cent). The majority of Jewish agricultural settlements had been established
as acts of Zionist policy in Palestine, and Communists
could hardly expect any success in these villages.

Jewish Urban Localities

The relative rise in the Communist vote, in 1961,
in all types of urban areas, was of a minor nature--from
2.15 per cent in 1959 to 2.39 per cent in 1961. Detailed
analysis of the data reveals, however, that the shifts were
not uniform.

The distinction between purely Jewish urban localities and mixed urban areas is forced on the student by the
occurrence of Arab minorities in the mixed cities and the
impossibility of definitely determining the weight of the
Arab vote therein. However, this distinction cannot serve
as the only relevant, or even the principal, factor in a study
of the Jewish Communist vote in the cities. One must distinguish between two sections of the Jewish electorate:
(1) the veteran firmly rooted population, whose support for
MAQI is negligible; and (2) immigrants at various stages of
absorption, which do not vary necessarily with the actual
year of immigration. Among the latter, there is slightly
more support for the Communists, although allowance must
be made for various factors such as the immigrants' lands

of origin, which may affect their voting behavior. It is also clear that the geographic distribution of new immigrants among and within different cities variously influences the patterns of the Jewish vote for MAQI.

Another criterion, partly implied in the previous one, is the size of the settlement and the composition of the population as divided between veterans and newcomers. New immigrants, for considerations of demographic and economic policy, are usually settled in development areas and medium-sized towns. Even immigrants of previous years whose economic position is still insecure continue to dwell in these areas or, if they live near large cities, tend to concentrate in separate localities or quarters--for example, Ma'abarōt (immigrant transition centers) which have become permanent immigrant settlements, and new housing estates built especially for new immigrants. Other immigrants, rather than settle in new immigrant villages, have preferred to use the financial assistance granted by the authorities to settle in or near the older cities.

Two main trends may be detected in the voting of a section of these immigrants: (1) there has been a rise in the Communist vote in certain places in Tel-Aviv, Haifa,

and Ramat-Gan which has had practically no influence on

the over-all Communist vote because of the relatively lower

weight of the immigrants in these cities and, a fortiori, of

that segment of economically backward immigrants which

votes Communist; and (2) in medium-sized and small cities

and in Ma'abarot, which have become immigrant settle-

ments, the presence of this segment is expressed in a

higher vote for the Communists.

Mixed Urban Centers

In this group are found the six cities described in

detail in Table 9. MAQI won 3.6 per cent of the total num-

ber of votes in these cities in 1961 as compared to 2.6 per

cent in 1959. However, these figures are merely an aver-

age of the Jewish and Arab vote, with the latter weighing

heavily in the scales. The Jewish Communist vote in these

cities was 2.3 per cent of the total number of votes in "Jew-

ish" polling stations. Thus, although the quasi-totality of

the population in these cities is Jewish, the vote in mainly

"Arab" polling stations increased the total percentage of

the Communist vote by more than 50 per cent. The rise in

the Arab Communist vote in the mixed cities in 1961 is also

noticeable in the comparison of the over-all Communist

vote in these cities with the percentage of MAQI votes in

the purely Jewish cities. The total number of votes in the

purely Jewish urban centers and the six mixed cities,

respectively, was almost equal. Nevertheless, MAQI

received in 1961 only 2.5 per cent of the votes in the for-

mer, as compared to 3.6 per cent in the latter; the com-

parative figures for 1959 were 2.2 per cent and 2.6 per

cent.

Our study of the election results in 53 polling sta-

tions in the six mixed cities where the bulk of the Arab vote

is concentrated revealed that in 1961 MAQI won 16.19 per

cent of the votes, as compared to 2.29 per cent in the other

polling stations. One may thus conclude that the Communist

vote was seven times larger in percentage terms in "Arab"

as compared to "Jewish" polling stations. In 1959, on the

other hand, only 9.09 per cent in the "Arab" stations voted

for MAQI as compared to 2.08 per cent in all the other sta-

tions in the mixed cities.

In general one can observe a rise of 80 per cent in
MAQI's vote in "Arab" polling stations, while the increase
in the other stations in the mixed cities approached a mere
10 per cent as compared to 1959. There was no uniformity
in the rate by which the "Jewish" vote as compared to the
"Arab" vote increased. Table 12 illustrates the changes
in the Communist vote in the mainly "Jewish" polling stations for 1959-1961.

In Jewish precincts in the six mixed cities, the Communist vote increased slightly in 1961, except in Lydda; its
order of rank was preserved.

The size of the "Jewish" Communist vote in Haifa,
Jerusalem, and Acre remained below the 2.29 per cent
"Jewish" average for the six mixed cities and below the
average Jewish Communist vote in all urban localities--
2.39 per cent (see Table 11). Tel-Aviv-Jaffa yielded a
slightly higher percentage than both these averages.

In explanation, it may be said that in Tel-Aviv-Jaffa,
Haifa, and Jerusalem, the majority of Arab residents live
in their own quarters, and it may be assumed that only a
few voted at "Jewish" polling stations. Furthermore, the

TABLE 12

PERCENTAGE OF COMMUNIST VOTES IN MAINLY JEWISH POLLING STATIONS IN SIX MIXED CITIES, 1959 AND 1961

City	MAQI's Percentage of Total Valid Votes in "Jewish" Polling Stations		Percentage of Total MAQI Vote in City Obtained in "Jewish" Polling Stations	
	1959	1961	1959	1961
Tel-Aviv - Jaffa	2.46	2.97	89.32	87.33
Haifa	1.87	2.30	62.65	51.97
Jerusalem	1.06	1.28	87.93	88.69
Acre	1.67	2.21	19.11	11.34
Ramlah	6.64	8.17	55.18	54.78
Lydda	4.22	3.88	79.95	56.36

Jewish population of these cities is composed principally of
veteran inhabitants and immigrants who settled there in the
early years of the State and are consequently well established.

1. Tel-Aviv-Jaffa. The Communist vote in 1961
was 2.9 per cent of the total number of votes cast in the
"Jewish" polling stations. The deviation from this average, both upwards and downwards, in the quasi-totality of
"Jewish" polling stations was not greater than 2 per cent
of all valid ballots. There were some stations where the
deviation was higher, the Communist vote reaching from 6
to 17 per cent of all votes. These deviations were concentrated in a limited number of precincts located largely on
the border between Tel-Aviv and Jaffa, rather dilapidated
in comparison with newer and richer residential areas, and
inhabited largely by new immigrants.[61] In all these stations
there was a sharp rise in MAQI's percentage as compared
to 1959. In addition, a marked increase also occurred in
some quarters that cannot be considered underprivileged.[62]
To sum up, the Communist vote in Tel-Aviv-Jaffa rose in

one-fifth of the polling stations, although this increase was, of course, not evenly distributed.

2. Haifa. The Communist vote was an average 2.3 per cent of the total valid votes in "Jewish" polling stations. The deviation from this average in most of the "Jewish" stations ranged between 1.5 and 2 per cent of the total number of votes. Only in 13 stations (out of 180, of which 160 were "Jewish") was the percentage of Communist votes higher, reaching 5 to 8 per cent. These stations, scattered through the city, are largely used by immigrants, not all of whom are newcomers, particularly in the suburbs of the "Lower Town."[63]

3. Jerusalem. The Communist vote was an average of 1.28 per cent of all the votes in the "Jewish" polling stations. The few stations in which the Communist vote was above the average were even less prominent than in the other two large cities. The highest Communist percentage in a "Jewish" station was a mere 5 per cent. Only 15 stations (out of 157, of which 150 were "Jewish") showed a noteworthy increase in the Communist vote. Almost all were in extremely poor sections on the Israel-Jordan

border[64] with dilapidated houses partly ruined since the
shelling during the 1948 Arab-Israeli War. Three of these
stations, however, are located in well-off residential
areas.[65]

4. Acre. The Communist vote was an average of
2.21 per cent of the total number of votes in "Jewish" polling stations. In only three of these was the Communist vote
higher than this average, reaching a maximum of 4.5 per
cent in one. The shift in the Jewish votes was also insignificant; only in four stations[66] (out of 22, of which 16 were
"Jewish") was MAQI's increase worthy of note. Acre is
largely an immigrant town, but the great majority came in
the early years of the State and is now well established.
The Jewish Communist vote appears to have come from
workers who have not yet been absorbed in the industrial
expansion of the city and are without permanent employment.

5. Ramlah. In Ramlah the Communists obtained
8.17 per cent of the votes in "Jewish" polling stations, the
highest Jewish vote won by MAQI in any mixed or Jewish
locality in 1961. Few stations showed a significantly lower
result in Ramlah, while in some the Communist vote

reached 12.1 per cent. The gain between 1959 and 1961 was also higher in Ramlah than in any of the other six mixed cities. This may be attributed to a steep rise in two "Jewish" stations, one of which was--significantly--in Ma'abara No. 3, where the Communist vote rose from 1.7 per cent in 1959 to 8.8 per cent in 1961. In contrast to other mixed cities, a not insignificant part of the Arab population of Ramlah is scattered in predominantly Jewish areas. This comparatively large Arab minority proved a suitable target for a concentrated Communist election campaign and must have exercised some influence on the size of MAQI's vote in preponderantly "Jewish" polling stations. In addition, the poor economic position of a section of the city's Jewish inhabitants, who are forced to seek employment outside its boundaries while living side by side with well-established older settlers, contributes to a relatively high protest vote. This is also reflected in a higher than usual vote for the right-wing opposition party Ḥerut.

6. Lydda. In Lydda the Communists obtained 3.88 per cent of all valid ballots cast in "Jewish" polling stations. Here, too, many Arabs voted in "Jewish" stations

and thereby probably increased the Communist vote, which was higher than in any other mixed city except Ramlah. Nevertheless, there was a slight drop in the Jewish Communist vote as compared to 1959.

Purely Jewish Urban Localities

Except for the occasional Arab vote in the "Jewish" polling stations in the mixed cities, similar tendencies are to be found in purely Jewish urban localities. This category includes cities, towns, and local councils, except for Moshavim (small-holder settlements), i.e., all purely Jewish localities of an urban, nonagricultural type. Among these there were 15 cities with more than 10,000 eligible voters each in 1961; the number of votes in each varied between 8,000 and 25,000, except for Ramat-Gan (near Tel-Aviv), which had some 45,000 votes. In 1961 a total of 255,758 votes, or over 60 per cent of all votes in purely Jewish urban localities, was cast in these 15 cities. The remaining 40 per cent of the votes were scattered among a large number of smaller towns and local councils.

Cities. Eleven of these cities[67] were founded well before the establishment of the State and have a sizable majority of veteran residents. In contrast, the other four cities[68] developed mainly after 1948 and have absorbed a large proportion of new immigrants. Thus one may expect dissimilar Communist support in these four towns and in the remaining 11.

In fact, the Communist vote in the 11 older cities varied between 1.2 and 3.4 per cent, thus ranging around the general average of 2.49 per cent in purely Jewish urban localities in 1961. The towns with the highest rate of growth, i.e., where the ratio of immigrants to old settlers was highest, had a higher than average Communist vote (Hertzlïya, Ramat-Gan, and Netanya). This fact supports, to a certain extent, the assumption that in Jewish urban localities the range of the Communist vote is frequently a function of the ratio between new immigrants and veteran residents. In Tiberias, the oldest of the 11 cities mentioned above, most new residents arrived in the early years of the State, and MAQI obtained only 1.2 per cent of the vote in 1961.

The four other cities, which developed mainly after
1948, show the effect on the Communist vote of differentia-
tions arising from the factor of economic absorption. New
immigrants were directed to Ashqelon and Be'er-Sheba in
accordance with the policy of scattering the population and
settling the Negev through direct and indirect economic
incentives. Many immigrants were provided with both
housing and steady employment. Be'er-Sheba also serves
as the administrative, economic, transportation, and education center of the Negev area and therefore has a number
of veteran residents. Many middle-class immigrants from
advanced Western countries have settled in Ashqelon.
These factors explain a low Communist vote, 1 per cent
and 1.3 per cent for Be'er-Sheba and Ashqelon, respectively, in 1961.

Holon and Bat-Yam present a different picture.
These cities, which border on Tel-Aviv, grew from a
nucleus of veteran residents but are now inhabited largely
by new immigrants, part of whom preferred to live near the
country's largest urban center even if this meant living in
temporary accommodations and commuting to work. The

Communist vote in these cities in 1961 was higher than the
average for purely Jewish urban localities, 4.3 per cent
and 6.4 per cent for Ḥolōn and Bat-Yam respectively.

In the majority of the 15 cities, the highest Communist vote came from areas which provided only temporary
housing for new immigrants or areas populated by immigrants who had not yet established themselves economically.
In Netanya, where the over-all Communist vote in 1961 was
2.6 per cent, MAQI achieved in the Shikkūn ha-Tzrīfīm
(Shack Quarter) 15.5 per cent, higher than even its 1959
percentage. In Petaḥ-Tiqva, 9.5 per cent voted for MAQI
in the immigrant quarter as compared to an average Communist vote of 2.3 per cent. A number of polls in Ma'abarōt
and former Ma'abarōt in Bat-Yam gave the Communists a
vote of 8.2, 10.3, and even 12 per cent against a general
average of 6.4 per cent.

The increase in the Communist share of the vote
from 1959 to 1961 in the 15 cities was higher than 0.5 per
cent in only four cities: Bat-Yam from 5.3 to 6.4 per cent,
Ḥolōn from 3.5 to 4.3 per cent, Bnei-Braq from 1.6 to 2.4
per cent, and Hertzlīya from 2.7 to 3.4 per cent. In nine

80

other cities the shift was from 0.1 to 0.5 per cent of the

total number of votes. Rehovot revealed no change; and in

Be'er-Sheba, MAQI's vote dropped from 1.6 to 1 per cent.

This picture confirms the explanations given for the

Communist vote in these cities. Bat-Yam and Holon, where

the Communist vote was highest, stood at the head of the

list of those with the largest increase in MAQI's votes. At

the other end of the scale were Be'er-Sheba and Ashqelon,

where the Communist vote, compared to 1959, fell by 0.6

per cent and rose by 0.2 per cent respectively. Rehovot

with no shifts should be included in the latter group. The

increase in the remainder of the 15 cities, less than 0.5

per cent, amounted to a mere handful of votes, often those

of a single family, and thus does not afford grounds for a

reasoned explanation. This observation also applies to the

shifts in Bnei-Braq and Hertzliya: with gains of 0.8 and

0.7 per cent respectively, the Communists obtained fewer

than 100 votes in each town.

Other Purely Jewish Urban Localities. In these

localities, i.e., those with fewer than 8,000 valid votes

each in 1961, two patterns of Communist voting emerged.

The first does not differ from the above-mentioned group of 15 purely Jewish cities; it concerns 28 smaller towns where the total number of votes varied between 2,000 and 8,000 (except for Eilat, Qiryat Mal'akhī, and Dīmōna where the total was slightly lower). The common feature of these towns is that the majority of their residents is employed in industry, crafts, and commercial and service occupations rather than in agriculture. Here, too, one may note the difference between localities populated principally by new immigrants and those where the majority are veterans or earlier immigrants. Ōr-Yehūda, populated solely by immigrants, gave MAQI the highest percentage in this group, 8.1 per cent in 1961, and as much as 11.9 to 13.4 per cent in some polling stations. The Communist vote was also above average in 'Azūr (6.8 per cent) and Ramat ha-Sharōn (6.6 per cent).[69] The former, also, is solely inhabited by new immigrants, some of whom are poorly housed, while the latter is a settlement which the influx of a large number of immigrants in recent years has changed into a town. The Communists received most of their Ramat ha-Sharōn votes from two polling stations in former Ma'abarōt and from a number of MAQI militants who have settled in the town, where the Communist Party maintains a rest home.

In most other localities in this group, the Communist vote was lower than the national Jewish average. Only in a few towns--Qiryat-Ōnō (4.6 per cent), Nesher (4.5 per cent), Nes-Tzīyona (4.2 per cent), and Yahūd (3.5 per cent)--was MAQI's percentage higher than the average in purely Jewish towns. Qiryat-Ōnō, for example, is an entirely immigrant town; in two of its seven polling stations MAQI got slightly more than 8 per cent, while its vote in the other stations was not far from the average.

The shifts of the Communist vote in these 28 towns, again, reveal the parallelism between the size of the vote and the extent of the shift. The Communists made the greatest gain in Ōr-Yehūda (from 6.9 per cent in 1959 to 8.1 per cent in 1961) and in Ramat ha-Sharōn (from 5.5 to 6.6 per cent); these were also the places with the highest Communist vote both in 1959 and in 1961. The rise in Communist strength was also relatively high in Beit-Shemesh (from 1.3 to 2.4 per cent), Qiryat-Motzqīn (from 1.5 to 2.4 per cent), and Nesher (from 3.8 to 4.5 per cent). A

rise also occurred in Qiryat-Shmone (1 to 1.6 per cent).
All, particularly Beit-Shemesh, are immigrant towns par
excellence. The shift in the other localities in this group
was a mere 0.5 per cent; and in three there was no change.
In Qiryat-Gat, a purely immigrant town enjoying full
employment due to its industrial development, MAQI's vote
even declined from 3.2 to 2.4 per cent.

The average Communist vote in these 28 towns was
2.56 per cent in 1961 as compared to 2.26 per cent in 1959.

A different pattern is apparent in the 40-odd agricultural settlements with fewer than 2,000 votes each (Hadar-
Ramatayim and Magdi'el are slightly larger). Here the
Communist vote was not only much lower than in other Jewish towns, but it actually dropped slightly in comparison
with 1959. MAQI received 1.40 per cent of the votes in
this group in 1959 and only 1.38 per cent in 1961. In effect,
the urban localities of an agricultural type constitute a separate group lying between the cities, on one hand, and the
villages, where the Communists made their weakest show-
ing, on the other.

In only 10 localities of this group, a quarter of the

total, was the Communist percentage in 1961 higher than

the average for the whole group (1.38 per cent), varying

between 2.1 and 6 per cent, though the number of Commu-

nist ballots in each of these 10 localities varied within the

narrow range of 17 to 65. The party won only isolated

votes in the other three-quarters of this group; it received

none in six of these settlements. In many of these settle-

ments, Communist strength declined as compared to 1959,

including one where the vote had been above the average of

the group. Since the figures concern a few dozen votes at

most, it is hardly possible to make any analytic generaliza-

tions. Nonetheless, one must note the presence of some

Communist votes in almost all these localities.

The scarcity of MAQI's support, which stands out in

these localities, in comparison to other urban localities

(see Table 13), may be explained by the essential character

of these localities and the general pattern of Israeli politics.

These are agricultural settlements of the private farming or

cooperative small-holder type. Agriculture in Israel has

flourished with the active encouragement of the authorities,

85

TABLE 13

PATTERNS OF COMMUNIST VOTE IN PURELY JEWISH
URBAN LOCALITIES

Type of Locality	Size in Valid Votes	Total Valid Votes 1959	MAQI's Percentage 1959	Total Valid Votes 1961	MAQI's Percentage 1961
15 large towns	8,000-45,000	240,700	2.21	255,758	2.67
28 medium towns	2,000- 8,000	106,070	2.26	109,299	2.56
Other Jewish localities (agri- cultural type)	Up to 2,000	40,159	1.40	39,480	1.38

and the settlements are generally prosperous and enjoy full employment. This, together with social homogeneity and a certain degree of conformity present in all small communities, explains the meagerness of the Communist vote.

CONCLUSIONS

We have focused our attention in this monograph on a description of the Communist vote and an attempt to analyze its motives as between ethnic communities and various types of localities in the elections to the Fifth Knesset. The voting patterns and motives in 1961 reveal, however, no substantial deviation from the other parliamentary elections held since the establishment of the State. An over-all glance at the period 1949-1961 indicates that the factors lying behind the Communist vote among Jews and Arabs respectively, as well as the voting patterns, have not undergone far-reaching changes.

Various elements motivated the Jewish Communist vote. An outstanding feature of the Israeli party pattern is its extreme lack of change despite a period of intensive immigration. All the parties in the political arena had existed at the time of the establishment of the State; even their relative Knesset and popular strength has remained fairly stable. Such shifts as have occurred have had no marked effect on the interparty balance.[70]

The ability of the established parties to absorb and integrate wave after wave of new immigrants, the failure of new immigrants to bring forth a leadership able to operate within a new social milieu, the monopolization of the possible political programs by the established parties--all contributed to the complete failure of attempts during the First, Second, and even later Knesset election campaigns to establish new parties representing the new immigrants or various Jewish ethnic groups. As a result, those groups of immigrants of various origins who sought material advantage were forced to act as pressure groups within or through the established parties.

With a difference, this is also true of MAQI. As a declared opponent of the established regime and unlike the other parties, MAQI was unable to promise and supply its supporters with jobs and housing. However, it could, and often did, offer the only possibility of a protest vote for that section of immigrants who had met with greater difficulties

in their early stages of adjustment. Many immigrants have

ceased to support the Communists after finding regular jobs

and housing, or after learning that support of MAQI would

not advance their integration into Israeli society. This

explains the turnover in the composition of the party and

in the extent of its support. The loyalty of the more or less

permanent nucleus of party supporters and members rests

mainly on ideological grounds. This group is composed

largely of immigrants from Eastern Europe, veteran Com-

munists or persons active in the regimes there, who left

because of anti-Semitism in their countries of origin or out

of disappointment with the changes and shocks of the post-

Stalin era.

The nature of the reservoir of Jewish Communist

voters also explains its concentration in the large and

medium-sized cities and its almost complete absence in

agricultural settlements. Most immigrants have settled in

urban areas; only a minority have been absorbed into agri-

culture, and even these have been within the framework of

existing Zionist settlement movements. The distinction

made between types of settlements reveals the fixed nature

of the Jewish Communist vote; in all Knesset elections this

vote has been primarily urban. The same voting pattern

was apparent in elections to the conventions of the General

Federation of Labor (Histadrut) in 1949, 1954, and 1959.[71]

To sum up: the Jewish Communist vote, including

insignificant zigzags and the slight rise in 1961, indicates

the stability of the limits of MAQI's strength as a marginal

factor on the Jewish political scene. In this relative stabil-

ity MAQI is similar to the other Israeli parties.

This is not true of the Communist vote in the Arab

community. Except for the drop in 1959, here one notes

growing Communist strength which reached its peak in the

elections of 1961. MAQI was, and remains, the party with

the second largest following among Israeli Arabs (except in

1959 when it fell to third place). The Communist Party has

consistently tried to serve not only as an instrument of eco-

nomic and local protest, but also--and mainly--as a means

of expressing the national frustrations, real or imaginary,

of this minority. Here, too, Communist strength is clearly

greater in the cities, partly because of the presence of a

politically conscious urban intelligentsia, a section of which sees in MAQI the image of a party that accords with their national-cultural frustrations. This is confirmed by the high Arab Communist vote in the elections to the Israeli Teachers' Federation in June 1962,[72] despite the fact that the Israeli Ministry of Education does not encourage the appointment of Communist teachers. Arab nationalists in Israel view MAQI, to a considerable degree, as an organization capable of aiding and abetting their feelings and hopes, and tend to ignore the social and economic doctrines of Communism. This stand is influenced and encouraged by the Soviet Union's penetration into the Middle East.[73]

It does seem that nationalism is no less influential than the economic factor in its impact on the Communist vote. This is borne out by the smallness of the Communist vote in the Jewish sector, despite the economic difficulties confronting new immigrants, and by its large volume among the Arabs, despite their prosperous conditions. The nationalist factor operates in opposite directions in the two communities; that the Israeli Communist Party is sensitive to the importance of this factor is not open to doubt.

NOTES

1. Two recent articles on the Knesset are: B. Akzin, "The Knesset," International Social Science Journal, XIII (1961), 567-582; and Scott D. Johnston, "Party Politics and Coalition Cabinets in the Knesset of Israel," Middle Eastern Affairs (New York), XIII (May 1962), 130-138.

2. An account of this election is given in E. Salpeter's "Israel Knesset Elections," Middle Eastern Affairs, XII (Nov. 1961), 262-268.

3. ha-Yarḥon ha-sṭaṭisṭi le-Isra'el (Israel Statistical Monthly), XII, Part I (Dec. 1961), 597.

4. Where sources are not indicated, the authors have computed the numerical data presented in this monograph.

5. No official history of the Communist Party in Palestine, written by one of its members, has yet been published. The two best accounts are G. Z. Isre'eli's M.P.S.--P.C.P.--MAQI--Qorot ha-miflaga ha-qomunisṭit be-Isra'el (M.P.S.--P.C.P.--MAQI--the Communist Party in Israel) (Tel-Aviv, 1953) and W. Z. Laqueur's Communism and Nationalism in the Middle East (2d ed.; London, 1957), Chap. VI.

6. M. Burstein, Self-Government of the Jews in Palestine since 1900 (Tel-Aviv, 1934), pp. 111 ff., 119 ff.

7. In 1920, Palestine had, according to British official figures, 589,177 Moslems, 71,464 Christians, 7,617 Druzes and others, and 83,790 Jews--cf. Encyclopaedia Hebraica (Jerusalem), VI (1956/7), 702; slightly different figures in J. Marlowe, Rebellion in Palestine (London, 1946), p. 59.

8. In the 1920's the P.C.P. published an Arabic periodical named Ilā al-amām (Forward). In 1944 it founded its Arabic organ--the weekly al-Ittiḥād (The Union). In 1945 a fortnightly for the Arab intelligentsia was added, al-Ghad (Tomorrow). In 1946 another Arabic weekly appeared, al-Mihmāz (The Spur). Cf. Y. Shim'ōnī, 'Arvei Eretz-Isra'el (The Arabs in Palestine) (Tel-Aviv, 1947), pp. 413-414.

9. Isre'elī, op. cit., pp. 100 ff., 120 ff. Cf. the Communists' own testimony in the matter, as collected by Shlomo Rekhav (pseudonym of Landqōtsh), Mifleget ha-hitkatshūt ve-gilgūleiha (The Party of Strife and Its Fortunes) (Tel-Aviv, 1956), pp. 27-32.

10. On the support of the Soviet Union for the creation of the State of Israel, and on its change of policy, see W. Z. Laqueur, The Soviet Union and the Middle East (London, 1959), passim; and K. Ivanov and Z. Sheynis, Gosudarstvo Izrail', ego Polozhenie i Politika (Moscow, 1958), passim.

11. There is but little printed information on MAQI during the first years of the State of Israel. See two

articles by M. Alexander (pseudonym) in Commentary (New York), "Israel's Communists and Fellow-Travelers," XIV (Aug. 1952), 136-144, and "Israel's Left Reels to the Shock of 'Prague,'" ibid., XV (April 1953), 379-389; B. Akzin, "The Role of Parties in Israel Democracy," Journal of Politics, XVII (Nov. 1955), 542-544; H. Niedermayer, "Die kommunistische Partei Israels," Zeitschrift für Geopolitik (Heidelberg), X (Oct. 1956), 5-10.

12. For further information on Israeli parties, their programs and composition, see M. H. Bernstein, The Politics of Israel (Princeton, 1957), chap. iii; J. Loewenson, "Physionomie des partis en Israël," Evidences (Paris), XI (Dec. 1951), 33-36; in greater detail, Akzin, in Journal of Politics, XVII (Nov. 1955), 507-545; and E. E. Gutmann, "Some Observations on Politics and Parties in Israel," India Quarterly (New Delhi), XVII (Jan.-March 1961), 3-29; also H. B. Sharabi, Government and Politics of the Middle East in the Twentieth Century (Van Nostrand Political Science Series, 1962), pp. 172-175.

13. ha-Yarḥōn ha-sṭaṭīsṭī le-Isra'el, XII, Part I (Dec. 1961), 599.

14. Ibid., pp. 597-599.

15. The last version of the party constitution was approved at the party's 14th National Congress in 1961; see mainly chap. vii, §44. The party constitution is appended to MAQI's report, ha-Veʿīda ha-arbaʿ ʿesre (The 14th National Congress) (Tel-Aviv, n.d. [1961]).

16. Laqueur, Communism and Nationalism in the Middle East, p. 118.

17. Ezhegodnik Bol'shoi Sovetskoi Entsiklopedii (1962), p. 252.

18. Taufīq Ṭūbī, a prominent member of MAQI, in a speech at the party's 12th National Congress, claimed that the ratio of MAQI's Arab members to its supporters in Knesset elections was 1:45! See MAQI's ha-Ve'ida ha-shteim 'esre (The 12th National Congress) (Tel-Aviv, 1952), p. 20.

19. MAQI's ha-Ve'ida ha-arba' 'esre, p. 112. It is impossible to verify this information, but it appears plausible compared to what one knows about the composition of the party and the structure of its committees.

20. Data from MAQI's ha-Ve'ida ha-shlosh 'esre (The 13th National Congress) (Tel-Aviv, n.d. [1957]), pp. 229-230; and its ha-Ve'ida ha-arba' 'esre, pp. 286-287.

21. ha-Ve'ida ha-arba' 'esre, p. 116.

22. According to the Census of May 1961, the total Jewish population was 1,932,357, of which 880,579 had immigrated since 1948; cf. State of Israel, Central Bureau of Statistics, ha-Tekhunot ha-demografiyot shel ha-okhlosiya (Demographic Characteristics of the Population; Population and Housing Census 1961) (Jerusalem, 1962), Part I, p. 10.

23. ha-Ve'ida ha-arba' 'esre, p. 110.

24. Qol ha-'am (MAQI's Hebrew daily), May 29, 1961.

95

25. ha-Veʻīda ha-arbaʻ ʻesre, p. 117.

26. On Jewish immigrants and their absorption in Israel, see S. N. Eisenstadt, The Absorption of Immigrants (London, 1954), passim, and "Cultural Assimilation and Tensions in a Country of Large-Scale Immigration: Israel," a collection of studies by A. Brodersen, A. Bonné, S. N. Eisenstadt, J. Ben-David, and J. T. Shuval, International Social Science Bulletin (UNESCO), VIII (1956), 7-123.

27. ha-Veʻīda ha-arbaʻ ʻesre, p. 117.

28. Calculated from the data in Central Bureau of Statistics, Statistical Abstract of Israel (Jerusalem), XII (1961), 46, 96.

29. It is possible that some of these immigrants, who have come from Eastern European "People's Republics," relate their personal economic problems in Israel to their nostalgia for their country of origin, and express this by joining or supporting MAQI. However, it seems that the influence of these factors weakens after the immigrants have been absorbed economically, socially, and otherwise.

30. ha-Veʻīda ha-arbaʻ ʻesre, pp. 113-117.

31. Statistical Abstract of Israel, XII (1961), 466; these data refer to persons aged 14 and over. The relatively high percentage of illiteracy among Israel's Jews is due largely to recent immigration from some African and Asian countries. Illiteracy among Israel's Arabs was much

higher at the end of the British Mandate, about 73 per cent--cf. Shim'onī, p. 389, based on British estimates at the time.

32. ha-Ve'ida ha-arba' 'esre, p. 111.

33. Bol'shaya Sovetskaya Entsiklopedia (2d ed.), XXVII (1954), 476.

34. Data in P. Dagan (ed.), Who's Who in Israel 1962 (Tel-Aviv, Dec. 1961), s.v.

35. Isre'elī, op. cit., p. 192, n. 2.

36. On Ḥabibī and his views, cf. W. Schwarz, The Arabs in Israel (London, 1959), pp. 142-144.

37. Dagan, op. cit., s.v.

38. Isre'elī, op. cit., p. 192, n. 2.

39. Cf. Miqunīs' speech in the report on MAQI's ha-Ve'ida ha-aḥat 'esre (The 11th National Congress) (Tel-Aviv, n.d. [1949]), Part I, especially pp. 20-21.

40. M. Sneh, Sheqī'at ha-Tziyonut (The Decline of Zionism) (March 1961), p. 4.

41. In evidence one may cite, i.a., a 468-page book on this subject, Shalom, shalom, ve-'ein shalom (Peace, Peace, There Is No Peace!) (Jerusalem, 1961). The author's pseudonym of A. Isre'elī is a cover for two MAQI members; cf. ha-Aretz (Hebrew daily) of Oct. 2, 1962, p. 2.

42. S. Miqunīs, 'Al ma loḥemet ha-miflaga ha-qomunisṭit ha-isre'elit? liqrat ha-beḥirot la-Knesset ha-sheniya (For What Does MAQI Fight? Towards the Elections to the Second Knesset) (Tel-Aviv, June 1951), p. 13.

43. S. Mīqūnīs, Ba-kinnūs ha-artzī shel Va'adei ha-meḥozōt u-mazkīrei ha-senīfīm shel MAQI (In the National Conference of MAQI's District Committees and Local Secretaries) (Haifa, 1955), p. 9.

44. MAQI's campaign platform for the Knesset, 1961.

45. On some of these limitations, see D. Peretz, Israel and the Palestine Arabs (Washington, D.C., 1958), Chap. VI.

46. For additional details, see J. M. Landau, "Die arabische Minorität in Israel," in J. M. Landau (ed.), Israel (Nürnberg, 1964), especially pp. 158-159.

47. No exact information is available on the circulation of these newspapers, but Taufīq Ṭūbī's claim in 1952 of 12,000 copies (ha-Ve'īda ha-shteim 'esre, p. 12) appears exaggerated.

48. S. Mīqūnīs, Be'ad Isra'el 'atzma'īt, demōqraṭīt, shōḥeret shalōm ve-qidma sōtzīyālīt (For an Independent, Democratic, Peace-Loving, and Social-Progress-Minded Israel) (n.p., March 1961): "The Central Committee has announced an I.L. 100,000 fund-raising campaign for MAQI's electoral campaign needs." Even if this sum (equivalent to $55,000 at the rate of exchange then prevailing) was collected in full--or a little more, as MAQI claimed--it could not possibly have covered all the expenses of MAQI's electoral campaign of 1961. One wonders where the balance of the money came from.

49. ha-Ve'ida ha-arba' 'esre, pp. 107 ff., especially pp. 110-117.

50. Qol ha-'am, July 19, 1961.

51. al-Ittiḥad, May 13, June 6, and June 13, 1961.

52. Ibid., Aug. 8, 1961.

53. ha-Yarḥon ha-staṭisṭi le-Isra'el, XII, Part I (Dec. 1961), 596.

54. Unless otherwise specified, all subsequent references to "votes" or "ballots" are to "valid votes" or "valid ballots."

55. J. M. Landau, "Les arabes israéliens et les élections à la Quatrième Knesset," International Review of Social History (Amsterdam), VII (1962), 28 and footnotes.

56. Nazareth, Shafa 'Amr, Ṭamra, Sakhnin, Umm al-Fahm, Ṭayyiba, Ṭira, Baqa al-Gharbiya, 'billin, Arraba, Kafr Yasif, Majd al-Kurum, Rama, Yafi', Ṭur'an, Raina, Kafr Qara', Kafr Qasim, Dair Ḥanna, Kafr Manda, Abu Snan, Judaida, Makr, Tarshiḥa, Buqai'a, Bi'na, Dair al-Asad, Naḥaf, Iksal, 'Ain Mahil, Kabul, Mu'awiya, Barṭa'a, Kafr Kanna, Mghar.

57. A sack-shaped strip near the center of Israel's border with Jordan.

58. For figures and examples, cf. Schwarz, op. cit., Chap. VII, especially p. 104. See also J. M. Landau, "A Note on the Leadership of Israeli Arabs," Il Politico Rivista di Scienze Politiche (Pavia), XVII (Sept. 1962), 625-632.

59. On MAPAM and its fortunes among the Arab electorate in Israel, see Y. Waschitz, "Arabs in Israeli Politics," New Outlook (Tel-Aviv), V (March-April 1962), especially 37-42.

60. In 1961, there were also 716 Arab voters living in Jewish urban localities and villages, where they constituted 0.09 per cent and 0.1 per cent of the eligible voters respectively.

61. E.g., the Florentine Quarter, ha-Kōvshīm Street, Yefet Street, and Jerusalem Boulevard.

62. E.g., Ramat-Avīv, Maʿōz-Avīv, and Aḥad ha-ʿAm--Yavne Streets.

63. E.g., Lower Haifa, Maḥane-Davīd, Qiryat-Ḥayīm, and Qiryat-Elīʿezer.

64. E.g., Muṣrāra, Baqʿa, Maʿabarat Talpīyōt, and Shmūʾel ha-Navīʾ Street.

65. E.g., Beit ha-Kerem and Qiryat-Shmūʾel.

66. E.g., Qiryat ha-Pelada and the settlement called ʿAmīdar Huts.

67. These cities, arranged according to the number of valid votes in 1961, are: Ramat-Gan (MAQI 2.8 per cent), Petaḥ-Tiqva (2.3 per cent), Bnei-Braq (2.4 per cent), Netanya (2.6 per cent), Givʿatayim (2.2 per cent), Reḥovōt (1.9 per cent), Rishōn Le-Tzīyōn (2.2 per cent), Ḥadera (2.2 per cent), Hertzlīya (3.4 per cent), Kefar-Saba' (2 per cent), and Tiberias (1.2 per cent).

68. Ḥolōn, Bat-Yam, Ashqelōn, and Be'er-Sheba.

69. The valid votes, in 1961, totaled some 2,100 in 'Azur and 4,500 in Ramat ha-Sharon.

70. See Akzin, op. cit., in Journal of Politics, and E. E. Gutmann, op. cit.

71. In the national elections to the Histadrut's Eighth Convention, MAQI obtained 4.9 per cent of the vote in the urban centers, 4 per cent in the Moshavōt (agricultural towns), and 0.7 per cent in the agricultural settlements--cf. the Histadrut's report ha-Ve'ida ha-shminit shel ha-histadrut (The Eighth Convention of the Histadrut) (Tel-Aviv), pp. 992-993. See also idem, ha-Ve'ida ha-shvi'it shel ha-histadrut (The Seventh Convention of the Histadrut) (Tel-Aviv), pp. 410-411, and the data of its Ninth Convention in its Qovetz statisti (Statistical Book of the Economic and Social Research Institute of the Executive Committee of the Histadrut), III (Tel-Aviv, Dec. 1959), 150 ff.

72. Cf. results in Hed ha-hinnukh (The Echo of Education) (weekly, Tel-Aviv), XXXVI (June 13, 1962), 3, and XXXVI (June 21, 1962), 19.

73. Some aspects of the relationship between Soviet policies and the politics of MAQI are mentioned by Scott D. Johnston, ''Communist Party Politics in Israel,'' in Robert K. Sakai (ed.), Studies on Asia 1964 (Lincoln, University of Nebraska Press, 1964), pp. 105-120.